CW00521662

A Glimpse
of Glory

My cancer survival story

R M PILGRIM

*"I shall not die but live
and declare the works of the Lord"
(Psalm118:17)*

ISBN-13: 978-1511971669
ISBN-10: 1511971665

All scripture quotations were taken from the King James Version (KJV) of the Bible. If this book has been a blessing to you, please email the author at **aglimpseofglory009@gmail.com**.

DEDICATION

I dedicate this book to my son Garvin, who encouraged and critiqued me while writing, and also to my beloved cousin Launa Bowman; who is such a wonderful and supportive person. For years she had been encouraging me to write. When I actually started she would often call from the United States to enquire how I was progressing.

I thank you both for your invaluable input into this project.

ENDORSEMENT

The author and I have been friends for over thirty years. When I was informed of her illness I decided to visit her. I took another friend along with me, and outside the room we met another person waiting to visit her.

Finally we were allowed to go in which was unusual for visitors in the ICU, but it was the divine work of God. I stood at her bedside looking down at her restless body going in and out of consciousness. At one point I called her name and said "Bridget is here." She opened her eyes and said "Bridget" and drifted off again. As I stood at her bedside this verse of scripture came to mind, *I shall not die but live, and declare the works of the Lord*–Psalm 118:17. I leaned over and repeated the verse a few times in her ears. We all prayed for her then left shortly after because our time was limited. I thank God today because he did honour his word. My friend is still alive and growing stronger in God as a result of her close encounter with death.

Sister Bridget Burke, 2015

ACKNOWLEDGMENTS

I thank God for healing me and allowing me a second chance to live.

To Dr Jorge A Dominguez, his surgical team who operated, and the nurses who worked tirelessly to ensure my recovery. I am extremely grateful, thank you all very much. Also, to the Churches, Pastors and other believers who prayed and gave financially and in-kind, a heartfelt 'thank you'.

To my family, I thank you all for your support. Special thanks to the members of Trinity Hall Ministries – my second family. Pastor Auguste, you have been extremely supportive; your reward will be great here on earth and in heaven. To all my close friends who visited me, prayed and contributed toward my needs, I thank you all. To the visitors who took a moment to encourage me, many thanks to you all.

R M Pilgrim 2016

PREFACE

I love the Lord with my whole heart. When I answered his call I worked assiduously helping as many people as I could. Who would have imagined that I would have fallen victim to Stage Three Colon Cancer, resulting in me living with a colostomy bag at my side?

It came as a shock to me and those who knew me working diligently in the Ministry. I then realised that sickness is no respecter of persons. It can happen to anyone.

I wrote this book to encourage and give hope to those diagnosed with cancer and their loved ones. CANCER IS NOT A DEATH SENTENCE. With faith in God, a proper diet and treatment one can overcome this disease.

R M Pilgrim 2016

CONTENTS

◉

1

TURNING POINT

During my teenage years, I was not a born again Christian but I had dreams of preaching the gospel to people, admonishing them to repent and prepare for the coming of the Lord. As time progressed in my early twenties, I met a Christian colleague at work and we became close friends. During her lunch break she would kneel and pray to God. On more than one occasion I joined her and would kneel next to her in silence. One day she loaned me a book entitled the "Rapture" that marked the turning point of my life.

A few days after having read the book I surrendered my life to the Lord. Instantly I became anxious to attend church, so I spoke to my younger sister Alma who lived a short distance from my home. In my conversation with her I expressed my interest in attending church and told her to call me on her way to service. As most young Christians, I questioned my decision – sometimes thinking maybe I had made a wrong choice. However, the Lord's call on my life won over the negative thoughts and I decided there was no turning back for me. I attended church a few times, then one night during prayer meeting when it was time for co-operate prayer, we all knelt down between the pews. While praying I heard an audible voice saying to me "I want you to be a missionary." I immediately looked up and turned around but all heads were bowed and everyone was deeply engrossed in prayer. I got up and sat down gripped with fear. When I got home that night I said, "Lord I don't want to be a missionary because they kill missionaries, why not a pastor or an evangelist?" Only when I attended Bible school I learned that a missionary with a direct call from God is an Apostle.

Many years elapsed and I kept thinking about the call of God. My two sons were very young and that was one of the hindering factors to me pursuing my calling. In 1992 I had a passionate desire to serve in the community. After speaking to an acquaintance about my intention, I was introduced to a political party. At that period the party was in search of a coordinator for the town of Saint George; although I had no experience in that field I took up the challenge. I was assured that I would be assisted by someone who once volunteered in that capacity. After communicating, we scheduled a time for work to begin. For reasons unknown, the person didn't show on several occasions. Due to this fact, I took the initiative to venture on my own. Knowing that fear is the enemy of success, I maintained a positive attitude. I trusted God for wisdom, and a successful first day in the field confirmed that I was capable. I was dedicated to my work, after my job on afternoons I would go straight out into the community. At times I left my children at home to attend the various meetings and functions the party hosted.

I didn't know my absence would be to the detriment of my family. My second son at an early age started experimenting with illegal substances and became very rebellious. I am pleased with the positive effect I've had on the lives of many, however it came with the price of a negative effect on my family.

Six years later I gained employment with the Party's office for a few months. A vacancy for the job of personal assistant to the Parliamentary representative for the town of Saint George presented itself, and I successfully attained it. I went from being a shy person who would not lift my hand in a meeting to ask a question, to a vibrant public speaker.

Whenever I travel through the town of Saint George, I can still see tangible evidence of the work that was done. I remembered when I was sent out by the minister to identify the work that needed to be done on Park Lane long step, the cobble stone alleys, and also the road on top the cemetery which was a muddy path way. I can recall the time the bulldozer started work on that road on top of the cemetery to the time the concrete road was completed. Even, after many years the road is still in good condition and serving its purpose.

In March of 1999 an evangelist from Trinidad visited the church that I attended. That Sunday morning when I arrived at church, there was no room inside to accommodate anyone, so I sat outside with other members. I vowed that I would be early for the night service. I got to the church promptly that night and sat close to the front row.

Coming to the conclusion of the service an altar call was made for people with calling on their lives. I said to myself, "I knew I had a calling on my life but I don't know if it is still there, however, I will go forward." When I got to the altar before I knew what was happening I landed on the floor. Based on the powerful operations in the service I knew the evangelist had the gifts of the spirit. That night many people fell to the floor (slain in the Spirit). When I got up from the floor my life was completely transformed.

In the following days the Lord began to speak to me about attending mission school. I knew the time had come to answer the call of God. After speaking to my pastor I gathered information about a school in Barbados called Youth-With-A Mission (YWAM). I applied to the school and was accepted. I was given a date by which I should leave the island. I also applied to the bank for a student loan but the process was handled at a snail's pace.

At one point I wondered whether I would be able to travel on the date assigned. Looking back now I can say it was a miracle.

One day before my departure the loan was approved. After seven years of service to the nation I had gained confidence and proper communication skills. I was now about to embark on a journey of faith. The last words which were spoken to me by a member of the party were: "If you work for God as diligent as you did for the party you will do well." In the Bible, when Abraham left his country he had no idea where he was going he only went by faith. Similarly I didn't know what was reserved for me I only obeyed.

◉

OFF TO MISSION SCHOOL

Life at campus was very different from anything I had been exposed to. It was a community where students and teachers lived on the base. Students came from regional and international countries. We had classes and chores, and on Sunday we visited different churches. The teachings of that School were life changing. My personal view then was if anyone went to YWAM and didn't change, there was very little hope of that person ever changing. As a result of the teachings, I developed an intimate relationship with the Lord that propelled me to rise early in the morning at 3am or 4am to commune with God.

I slunk to the gardens pouring my heart out to the lord with tears running down my cheek. I often thought about my children and I would habitually go to the cane fields in the back of the school to scream my frustration away. I still scream! If I am feeling down I shout hallelujah! I feel better when I scream as the bioenergetics exercise allows me the release I need. Approaching the conclusion of the course we were preparing for outreach.

That Sunday morning we visited a church where the pastor was also a prophet. An altar call was made for the entire class so we stepped forward. The prophet began praying for us, and then he pointed his finger at me and proclaimed "I see you, I see you writing, and you will reach most of the nations with your writing."

I will never forget that prophecy. I always loved writing. During my school years, I took part in essay competitions. When I was a student at Barbados Bible College I discovered my ability to write poems. Since then I have written numerous poems and they are just lying on a shelf. I believe one day I will publish them.

OUTREACH IN GUYANA

Following that Sunday plans were in high gear for our outreach programme. The class was divided into two groups, one group to travel to Guyana and the other to Suriname. I was happy to be placed in the group travelling to Guyana because of the language barrier in Suriname. While in Guyana we ministered through drama, dance and preaching: this included schools, churches and homes for the aged. We also did personal evangelism, going around the villages in pairs spreading the gospel. One day we were sent out to do a questionnaire in pairs. Steve, my teammate and I started following a muddy pathway. We crossed over eight streams. I was clad in sneakers and socks with water way over my ankles. We had no idea where the road path was going to lead us.

We spotted a small house in the distance; we then doubled our steps as we became curious. To our surprise a man was sitting bare back on the porch of that house surrounded by water. When he saw us approaching he went inside and dressed appropriately then returned to greet us. We said hello and told him who we were. At that point I felt moved to share my testimony with him. Steve also shared his testimony and encouraged him. After listening to us he felt comfortable to share his frustration. He started opening up to us, telling us how lonely he was. His wife had taken their two children and moved in with a male companion. He was not allowed to see the children and that made him very unhappy. He was contemplating what he should do when we showed up. After he was finished telling his story we prayed for him, then invited him to church in the village where we were having night service. Days following we got news that the man got a job and things had improved for him. God led us to him at the right time. This reminds me of the widow and Elijah in the book of 1Kings 17:7-16, she was going to eat her last meal with her son while awaiting death caused by famine. God was looking on all the time and he had a plan. She gave the prophet of her last meal and God multiplied the little which she had and she was fed throughout the famine. When that man thought all hope was gone, God sent us to him. The encouragement he received motivated him to step out in faith then help was made available to him. After twenty five days of ministry in Guyana it was time to return to Barbados.

We got back to Barbados and everyone's focus was going home. It was about that time the Lord spoke to me and said, "Remain in Barbados for another two weeks." I said, "Lord where will I stay," and he gave me the name of a sister who was a member of a church close to the school. I knew her as I attended a 5am prayer meeting which she held. The following day I prayed and went to her house and told her what the Lord had said. Without hesitation she told me I was welcome to stay at her home.

I called her mom (she is now deceased). In mom's house a week of fasting was in progress and I joined the group. At the end of that fast the Lord visited us during the night in a mighty way. I was lying on my bed and I suddenly felt like a high voltage of electricity was permeating my entire being and my body shook violently. After that experience, whenever I prayed for people who were demon possessed the demons would leave. If they had a desire to receive the Baptism of the Holy Spirit and I lay hands on them, immediately they would receive the Holy

Spirit evidenced by them speaking in unknown tongues.

Mom saw the hand of God on my life and she always encouraged me. She was the first person to give me an opportunity to preach in open air meetings. As the missionary President of her church she had a passion for souls and was a prayer warrior and a positive influence to all those around her. Her life blessed so many including mine, I feel confident that we would one day be reunited in glory with our God. The two weeks went by and I was thankful for the anointing the Lord had placed on my life, and for the goodness he had shown me while away from home. It was now time for my departure. On my return to Grenada, I was delighted to be united with my children. Christian brethren heard that I was back in the island and contacted me. I became active in prayer meetings where there was always a great move of God.

I remained in Grenada for a few months then travelled back to Barbados and got married to a Christian brother I met on one of the outreach missions. He was my best friend; smart and intelligent and most of all he treated me with dignity. During that period the Lord spoke to me about continuing my theological studies. I learned of Barbados Bible collage so I enrolled with the School. After a few months the studies were becoming burdensome to me, and then I was made aware of a new Christian University which opened its doors with its main focus being the anointing and the gifts of the Spirit. A friend had started attending the university and the reports coming out aroused my interest.

Weeks later I transferred to the university, I saw the power of God demonstrated in our classes in a way I had never witnessed before. After two years I had completed my associate degree and was studying for my bachelor's degree.

I was in the habit of regular fasting and during the month of May in 2003 for three weeks I wept before God for reasons unknown. While fasting, I had a vision where I saw my husband's body being taken out of the house on a stretcher. Following that dream, I became perturbed considering the susceptibility of my husband who was a victim of substance-abuse before his conversion to Christianity. Many times he would say to me "Rea, you deserve better."

I never argued when he came home late; I was always indulgent. Years after we got married he approached me and said, "I want to ask you a question, are you an angel? I have been watching you for years and no one can pretend for so long." I will always remember those words because I knew it was God's grace and all the credit I had to give to God. At times when he became discouraged, he would read his Bible, sing and worship God. His favourite song was "Be magnified."

One Sunday morning the radio was broadcasting and a local preacher came on. During the course of his message he said, "If someone commits suicide that does not mean he/she will go to hell." I hoped that my husband was not listening to the preacher, however, it turned out that he was. The same week before he died he was walking on the side walk close to home and a stone from a passing truck almost landed on him. In another instance he was riding a bicycle and he lost control landing him over a wall. I will never forget that Thursday night when my husband came home, a deep sleep suddenly came over me preventing me to sit up and speak to him as I usually did. The Friday morning I was awaken approximately 5am with the tragic news that my husband was found dead. At that moment I became numb realising that he ended it all. Forthwith, the preacher's sermon came back to my mind.

There are many people who are vulnerable out there grappling with problems and are looking for solutions, or a way out of their misery. Many times as human beings we are plagued with problems some stemming from our childhood and others that happen to us along the way.

It is better to pray for people that are victims of circumstance than to condemn them, because the end product is what we see but the root cause is always invisible. It was not an easy time for me, but my in-laws and good friends stood with me and supported me. My husband had a passion to work with people that were victims of substance abuse to help them recover. He had many brilliant ideas but didn't live to establish them. At his funeral included in the eulogy I wrote was a promise never to let his vision die, but to ensure they become a reality someday. Following the funeral I didn't return to Grenada immediately, but continued working with a Christian School. By then I had dropped out of the university. Months later the university wrote asking me to return to complete the course. I wrote back declining politely. Years later I received information that the university had closed its doors.

Coming to the end of 2003 I received an invitation by email to be a guest speaker in a Christian Retreat in Grenada. I accepted the invitation and travelled to Grenada. While on the island I had a vision where I saw a large gold slab on the ground with the name of Jesus written on it, sadly, Jesus' name was covered with soil. I knew that was not a good sign for Grenada.

There was nothing I could have done but pray for my beloved island. After the retreat I returned to Barbados. Towards the end of 2003 the Lord started speaking to me about returning to my home land. In 2004 my mind was all made up. I then discussed the matter with my boss who was very understanding. In July of that year I returned to Grenada.

◉

2

VISIONS OF DEVASTATION

It took me a while to settle down, coming from a country where transportation was easily accessible from 5am in the morning to midnight seven days a week. I had to get acquainted with a transportation system which was only available about thirteen hours a day and six days a week. As the days progressed I was experiencing difficulties in getting break through during prayer. I knew something was wrong in the nation.

Between the end of August and the beginning of September, I had two visions. In the first one I saw the earth like a globe and two angels standing one to the centre, and the other stood close to latitude 12.05 where Grenada is located and pointed at it. He looked at the angel at the centre and that angel gestured by the raise of his hands in agreement. A few days later I had the second vision where all the trees had lost their leaves and they became brown in colour. The houses were without roofs and the island looked like a dump heap. Coming out of that vision I said to myself "That cannot happen here." Around the fifth of September I was made aware of a storm in the Atlantic basin named Ivan whose strengthening was unprecedented at such a low degree. It was forty-nine years since Grenada was hit by Hurricane Janet. The young generation had no knowledge what a hurricane entailed. When the hurricane watch was broadcast on the radio very few took warning. Some people said things like "God is a Grenadian; no storm is coming here." By September 6, Ivan appeared to be heading to Barbados. Some Grenadians felt at peace, but there were others who monitored to see if it would change course.

THE IMPACT OF HURRICANE IVAN

September 7 came, there was a breadfruit tree behind my house and some neighbours came by to pick. Little did they know, they were picking the final breadfruits that tree would ever produce. The day began as a normal sunny day, after midday a gradual transition took place, with the weather alerting us that Ivan was definitely approaching. I was at home with my two sons listening to the radio for up-dates. There was a misunderstanding between them: Bren kept changing the station and Garvin told him to leave the radio on one station. Bren failed to comply so Garvin walked out and went to a neighbour's house.

A few hours after Garvin left, we were still listening to the radio and I heard that Ivan was headed directly towards us. I remembered someone told us we were sheltered down in the valley with lots of wind breaks. After 2pm the wind began to blow with high gust, the Breadfruit, Golden Apple and French Cashew trees fell, and then the windbreaks began falling one by one. As the wind intensified the galvanize over my room lifted and water started coming in, so I grabbed all my books and clothes that were hanging and stuffed them into a suitcase. By that time Bren had a hammer trying to nail down the galvanize. He needed assistance but I was unable to reach the roof; he struggled and became frantic as the wind was howling while Ivan blasted the island. I was standing in front of the door and the glass in the window was shattering sending splinters everywhere, I froze and couldn't move. Bren saw me standing in danger and shouted, "Mom move!" He pulled me away and I followed him inside the bed room. He placed a mattress on the floor and we sat with our backs against the wall and the mattress served as a protective barrier.

While we were sitting I believe the wind could have been over one hundred and twenty-five miles an hour. The house began to shake violently on all sides. In my mind I said, "I wonder where we will end up?" I heard the house breaking up then suddenly we found ourselves sailing away with the flooring! It stopped about thirty-five feet from the original foundation. Part of the house went into the main road, and the other part went over into the neighbour's property. Thank

God I only received a scratch from broken galvanize and a piece of lumber fell on my right hand. My son had no injury. I looked up from the ground and realised that a coconut tree was swaying over our heads. Roofs were flying everywhere. I can recall pulling a suit case close to me and putting a bath towel over my head.

When I looked I said "Bren! Tornado!" he looked up and saw what I had seen. We were at the mercy of the elements. On the ground I prayed and cried out to God, but Ivan continued pounding the country.

We remained on the ground for hours, then came a calm. We got up and looked around. All the roofs on the surrounding houses were off. We climbed over piles of debris. The skirt I was wearing split from bottom to top but luckily I was wearing leggings. We continued trying to get to civilisation and help! Finally we saw a light coming from the downstairs of one of our neighbour's house. When we got there the place was filled with people. I was given a change of clothing, and then I sat down hoping for the best. Bren had a small video camera; so he went outside trying to capture whatever he could. The rain came down heavily while he was filming and it affected the camera; he came back that night disappointed.

The following morning we left the neighbour's house and walked to the place where our home once stood. Everything I owned was scattered about the yard. My beautiful clothing was in the mud, stove, refrigerator, TV and wares were in the yard. As I stood there pondering, it dawned on me that I was homeless for the first time in my life. Moments later Garvin returned from the neighbour's house. He stood in shock as the dreadful sight rendered him speechless. Even more shocking were the words spoken to break his transient silence. With composed tranquility he said he had another place to live and he left. Bren and I were neglected, left to manage on our own.

The community was draped in despondency as the radio stations were not functional, and there was no communication from the authorities who were perhaps suffering equal shock. After Ivan I spent two nights by a neighbour, and then was made to travel to a friend's house every night for two weeks, accompanied by Bren who guaranteed my safety. Bren along with neighbours, laboured persistently to repair our home.

During the ensuing days we finally got the help needed as I was able to contact friends in Barbados who sympathised and assisted tremendously. One afternoon Garvin returned and the euphoric feeling of having him back was overwhelming. Immediately after he returned, he took up his tools and displayed his workmanship. In less than two days the pending work on the house was completed. Grenada received help regionally and internationally. According to the news release at that time, 90% of the homes were damaged, 39 persons lost their lives and damage of 1.1 billion dollars was estimated. We are a very resilient people and were able to rebuild in record time. The vegetation is now green and flourishing and I pray it will remain that way for a very long time.

In 2005 there was a sudden change in Bren's attitude which Garvin and I found difficult to deal with, as he was incessantly disrespectful. One year after my return I moved out of the house. A colleague accommodated me until I found an apartment. A few months later Garvin also moved out and shared an apartment with a friend.

3

MINISTRY ESTABLISHED

In November of 2004 I was ordained as a Pastor, but I continued to attend the church where I fellowshipped every Sunday. My son used to say to me, "Since you came back you have not started any ministry." But my reply was always "I cannot start anything unless the Lord gives me the green light." In January 2005 I was invited to a Pastors' conference, and the main speaker was from Barbados.

During his message the Lord spoke directly to me and I knew this was the confirmation I was awaiting. All the information I needed to establish the ministry was saved in my computer while I was in Barbados, including the name which I received after four hours of prayer. Following the conference, the Lord spoke to me about hosting a day of Prayer in Windsor Forest. After discussing it with my prayer partners, I visited the owner of the disco in Windsor Forest and requested the use of the building to host the prayer meeting for that Saturday. The owner had no objection to my request. We went full speed ahead with all arrangements for the prayer service. My two main petitions to God were: a church for Windsor Forest and the rebuilding of the Saint David's town.

The prayer meeting was a great success and it was well attended. Approximately one year and some months later a church was established in Windsor forest. One day I took hold of a newspaper and while reading through it, I noticed an article stating that a developer had commenced work in the La Sagesse area and new roads were being opened. On my way to Grenville sometime later, I noticed that work was indeed in progress and that made me very happy, but due to an economic crisis work ceased. I still continue to pray that one day a town will be built in Saint David's and it will not be referred to as "the virgin parish" or "the parish without a town." Saint David's once had a town called Megrin which was established in 1609 and destroyed during the 1795-96 Fedon conflict and the town was never rebuilt.

In March 2005, Trinity Hall Ministries opened its doors for the first time in Tanteen. We were few in number but the power of God was mighty delivering people from demon possession during the services. One Sunday morning after church a resident close to our meeting place came to see me complaining that we were disturbing him from his rest. Our service commenced at 10am. At that time we didn't have a public address system, but utilised a battery operated key board. To avoid further contention I apologised to him. He was the kind of person that would stop at nothing to achieve his desires. Shortly after that encounter we were given notice to vacate the premises. We were told that there was a need to renovate the building. At that time I began seeking the Lord aggressively. Being the founder of the ministry it was my responsibility to locate another building. One day while travelling on a bus to the city, the Lord showed me a building and said to me "go and ask for it." I looked in astonishment and said, "Lord that is a cinema." The Lord said for the second time "go and ask for it." With no hesitation when I got to the nearest bus stop I alighted from the bus, and walked briskly towards the cinema. Entering through the front door I noticed the owner was standing in the centre of the aisle. I greeted him and told him the reason for my visit. After listening to me his exact words were "The cinema is there, you can use it, and you all can start right away." After leaving the building I was very excited to share the good news with the members of our church.

Keeping a worship service in a cinema was not a traditional practice; as a result we were met with lots of criticism. However, I remained focused knowing I did not choose that place on my own accord. In my effort to reach the nation I approached a radio station and was met by a young Christian man who hosted a programme every Sunday. He agreed to allow me a half hour on his programme to share the gospel. Through the broadcast, people locally, regionally and internationally received spiritual help. While in prayer in 2005 the Lord told me he had placed me in the office of the apostle, and one year later in 2006 He told me to stand in the office of the apostle. Knowing that people misunderstood the office of the apostle, I took no action in announcing this to the congregation.

By 2006 the ministry was well established with outreach in other parishes. During that year I travelled to Trinidad for the first time for six days. I was hosted by a couple who were both pastors. I had a wonderful time worshiping God with the brethren and I also preached one night. I had the privilege to view some of the historical sites including the pitch lake. I went shopping one day, to purchase gifts. I always enjoy shopping whenever I travel and look forward to it. An escalator is something I am not fond of. On the morning of my departure, to check in I had a choice to use the stairs or escalator and I chose the stairs. I was late for my flight that morning; the other passengers were already aboard the plane. After checking-in, it was time to exit to board the plane. This time I had no choice, the escalator was before me. I took a deep breath and stepped on. When I got to the bottom I was thankful. Many years prior I got stuck in an elevator. Since then I always prefer the stairs.

September 2006 I was in one of our Wednesday morning prayer meeting and I heard the Lord say these words to me: "Today is the beginning of your Healing Ministry." I know the Lord always speaks to me and what he says comes to pass. Minutes later a lady came through the door with a knee problem and she began praising the Lord. Then the power of God came upon her and the first healing took place that morning, this lady was jumping up and down shouting, "I am healed I am healed".

Coming to the close of 2006 I was made aware that many marriages were in crisis. In an effort to strengthen marriages I sought sponsorship from the private sector and hosted a seminar for married couples, and for couples who were engaged to be married entitled "A TOUCH OF LOVE." The main criteria were twofold: (i) To strengthen the fabric of the society which is the family and (ii) To raise funds to purchase vital supplies for the ministry. I did this out of a heart of love and compassion. Even though the seminar was advertised on radio, it was poorly attended. Those who attended were very appreciative of the knowledge imparted to them. The cameraman told me he found the seminar was very informative and he was disappointed that more couples did not participate.

In 2007, my cousin Launa Bowman (Sister Bowman) came for a vacation from the USA, bringing with her barrels of foodstuff and clothing to distribute to the less fortunate. She has a gift for personal evangelism, and the occasions when we went out to distribute tracts I was so impressed with her presentation that most of the time I kept silent and just listened. We travelled to Carriacou one morning by boat to distribute tracts. No one could have anticipated the peril we would have had at sea. When we got close to the Kick-em-Jenny active volcano, the waves became boisterous. The boat began tossing to and fro; passengers became frantic, sliding off their seats while others began vomiting. We feared whether we would make it to Carriacou alive. The boat appeared as if it would smash to pieces. My cousin was so terrified that she called her pastor in Virginia, USA and requested prayer for our safety. As we got closer to port the sea became calm and passengers were once more in high spirits preparing to disembark. Upon arrival we went out to the villages speaking to people about the Lord and handing out tracts.

That day a few people made decisions to serve the Lord including a young man named Ivan. We laughed when he said his name remembering the devastation caused by hurricane Ivan. I also remarked that no one should consider naming a child Ivan. In the afternoon we had lunch in one of the restaurants in the capital Hillsborough, and prepared for our journey back to the main land. During Sister Bowman's stay we hosted a crusade at the Ravine Disco in Windsor Forest. Days before the crusade, new batteries were inserted in the Bull Horn (megaphone) and we drove around to advertise the crusade. I was speaking at the top of my voice for miles. We got to a certain area where men sitting by the roadside were asking "What you all having?" and we stopped and told them. All that time we were not aware that the Bull Horn was not working. When we did find out all we could have done was to laugh.

The crusade was very successful. We had a live Christian band, and many people attended: some people surrendered their lives to the Lord. Following the crusade we had a fun day in Camerhogne Park close to Grand Anse beach. We had lots of eats and drinks including "Oil Down" (Grenada's national dish) which is made from breadfruit and coconut primarily. After eating we enjoyed bathing in the world famous Grand Anse beach. After that eventful day it was now time for my cousin to prepare for her departure. Upon her return to the US she invited me to visit with her. I travelled to the US in January

2008. She travelled from Virginia to New York to meet me so we could travel back to Virginia together. We stayed with her sister in New York. It was very cold at that time but I enjoyed the winter. It was always my dream to experience winter, so when I landed in the US I was overwhelmed with joy, it was a dream come true. After a few days we travelled to Virginia.

My time was spent attending church, visiting family and friends, and sometimes we would go shopping. I had three speaking engagements at church mainly organised by Launa. I had a wonderful and adventurous holiday. My cousin and her sons made me very comfortable in their home. At the end of the five weeks we returned to New York and from there I returned home.

The years that followed I continued working in the ministry. In December 2010 Bren was incarcerated. Two months later Garvin and I returned to our home in Independence Avenue.

○

4

GREAT EXPECTATIONS

In 2011, six years after establishing Trinity Hall Ministries, I felt quite energetic and anticipated maximum success for that year. Sickness or set backs were not entertained in my mind; I was working feverishly and doing well. I never envisage that anything would go contrary to my expectations. Apart from my service in Trinity Hall Ministries, I kept busy at home in Independence Avenue with my backyard gardening. That year I purchased the necessary tools and gears from the hardware store to facilitate my work. With the help of my first son Garvin, the soil was prepared for planting. A variety of short term crops were planted including: peas, corn, okras, sorrel, sweet potatoes and yams. After a couple of months I was fully prepared to harvest some of my crops. I had enough to share with family, friends and neighbours, and still kept a reasonable supply for myself. I believe my interest in farming came about from my early childhood book "Nola on the Farm" and also by being a part of my school's 4H Club of which gardening was an integral part.

In August of 2011, four years after the Lord told me to stand in the office of the apostle, a prophet was sent by God to our Ministry. He addressed me as Apostle in the presence of my congregation. I remembered asking him how he knew my calling. That same Sunday I was released from the Pastoral office, I was anointed and prayed for by the Elders to prepare for my first missionary journey. Pastor Auguste was appointed as the new Pastor of the church. She had to see to the smooth functioning of the ministry in my absence. Just prior to the planned trip I had some dreams that were rather disturbing. In the first dream I saw a woman on a hospital bed but her face was not visible. This dream was repeated on several occasions. In the second dream a few men dressed in black robes came to bury me. I quoted Psalm 118:17 KJV: *I shall not die but live and declare the works of the Lord.* When I said those words the men vanished from my presence, but they left the coffin behind. I shared the dreams with close family and friends but the interpretations were not known. These dreams were warning signs for me, but at that time I was not aware that the woman in the dream was me. In September of that same year a couple in our ministry was scheduled to travel, so I volunteered to stay with the children in their absence. Half way through their vacation I noticed I was becoming exhausted while carrying out my duties, but I thought I needed some rest. When the couple returned I went home to prepare for my trip.

During the month of October I purchased a one year ticket to travel to Barbados. I met a good friend in the city that day. While walking we began discussing my upcoming missionary trip. She was shopping for shoes and I accompanied her to a few stores. After a diligent search she found something suitable. We said our goodbyes and she headed over to the Carenage which is sometimes called the waterfront. At the end of October we had two major events in Church: Water Baptism and a Wedding. A couple was receiving counselling while the candidates for baptism were being prepared in converts' class. Finally the Saturday arrived and we were on our way to Annandale Waterfall for the baptism. In less than forty minutes we approached the drive way of the waterfall. After the vehicles were safely parked, we alighted and assembled under one of the sheds. A mini service was conducted wherein the candidates were all given the opportunity to testify of their Christian experience. After the singing of a few hymns and a brief exhortation, it was time to take our journey down to the waterfall. It was a beautiful area often visited by tourist. The sulphur spring was flowing on the left, and the golden lining on its trail could not be ignored. As we descended the steps, the waterfall cascaded about fifty feet below forming a vast pond. The baptism commenced and the candidates were helped into the water one by one, while the rest of the members sang choruses. At the completion of the baptism we ascended the steps and headed for the changing area. After making sure that everyone was dressed and ready, we boarded the vehicles and journeyed to our various destinations.

The Sunday was a special service, the candidates that were baptised, were taken into fellowship as new members. It was a time of refreshing in the presence of the Lord. The service concluded an hour earlier to facilitate the wedding which was a simple ceremony comprised of family and close friends. They all were assembled to witness the exchange of vows. After the benediction the bridal party proceeded to the reception. It was already late in the afternoon and I was very anxious to get home.

SYMPTOMS OF ILLNESS

I felt discomfort in my abdomen shortly after arriving home. I thought I may have been constipated so I took a laxative. I waited a few hours but there was no sign of a bowel movement, so I went to bed. At about midnight I awoke vomiting profusely, with excruciating abdominal pains. I had no explanation for why this was happening to me. Garvin also awoke and was concerned about my condition. Minutes later when the vomiting ceased, I went back to bed.

On the Monday morning I made no attempt to visit a physician, I thought maybe it was gastroenteritis. During that day I felt very sick and was unable to stand in the kitchen to prepare a meal. Garvin had left for work early that morning while I was still in bed. I prayed and waited for him to come home to take me to the emergency room. My second son Bren was in confinement at that time so I had to depend on Garvin for the assistance that I needed. Being a widow, my children mean a lot to me. I cannot imagine what life would have been without them. That evening when he arrived home I told him what I have been experiencing during the day, and my need to seek medical assistance. After dinner he immediately got ready and we left for the hospital. Although the hospital was within close proximity the discomfort I felt made it appeared as a longer distance. I felt the sudden change in gear as the car mounted the Grand Etang road and within minutes we were there. After speaking to the nurses at the desk, I was ushered into the examination room to be seen by a doctor.

A female doctor proceeded to attend to me. The way in which she spoke to me made me wonder whether I was a patient or a detainee. I was praying that this whole ordeal be expedited, so I could leave that room. This was the first time I had witnessed such demeanour in a professional. One part of me felt like walking away from her, but in my condition I had no choice but to remain. Finally I was given some prescriptions and was told by the doctor to "Go home and eat." The following morning I sent to purchase the medication and started taking them right away. While I waited for improvement in my health, I was constantly praying and occasionally thought of my missionary trip to Barbados. Arrangements were being made to accommodate me, and the brethren were anxiously awaiting my arrival. Tuesday evening came and there was no improvement in my condition, that night I had very little sleep. When I woke up Wednesday morning, I made a decision to go to Sister Allen's home, a member of our Church. I knew then that I needed help because my son was working late hours. I got to Allen's home in the afternoon where a room was already prepared for me. I was given a cup of hot tea which I drank, then took my medication. It was now evening, the shadows began to fall and the sun was seen sinking in the horizon with radiant beauty.

The pains began to intensify so I went into the room and lay down. The radio was tuned to Harbor Light Gospel Station and violin music was being played. To escape the intensity of the pain, I pictured myself worship dancing dressed in a white flowing gown on a huge stage. I used the stage beautifully and moved gracefully. It was a moment of exuberance- a moment that I will always reminisce on.

Reality struck me when the pains became almost unbearable. I grabbed hold of my cellphone and dialed Garvin's number. I said, "Son please come and take me back to the hospital." It was already close to midnight. In a matter of minutes I saw the car lights beaming as he raced up the hill towards the house. I was already moving down the steps when the car came to a halt. I opened the door and sat in the front seat then fastened my seatbelt. The engine was set in motion; we were on our way. This time, a male doctor was on duty at the hospital. This was a great relief for me after my previous encounter with the female doctor. This doctor was very kind and polite; he kept me overnight and did all the necessary examinations. During the night I lay there oblivious of the root cause of my illness. In the reception area Garvin was anxiously awaiting my results. Whatever was the cause of my condition I knew I had to fight with all my strength, because I did not want to die before fulfilling my purpose here on earth. At 5am I was released from the emergency room and was told by the doctor to be at the X-ray Department by 7am. I then called my son from the reception area. He advanced towards my direction, looked at me with enquiring eyes and asked, "What did the doctor say?" He was very concerned but there was not much to tell because the doctor was tight lipped. On our way home we stopped at a gas station mini mart. I remained in the vehicle while Garvin purchased a cup of hot tea. When he returned I quickly drank some of it, before it got settled in my stomach I started vomiting again. We drove to Sister Allen's house where she was given an update on my condition. I only had time for a quick shower and changed and Garvin and I headed to the x-ray department. By that time Pastor Auguste was informed and without hesitation she joined me at the x-ray-department. I sat restlessly in the waiting area in pain, anxiously awaiting my turn. Suddenly I heard my name. I immediately got up and proceeded towards the entrance. I was then ushered into a changing room to prepare for the x-ray. I made my way towards the radiologist. A chest x-ray was done, and as I was heading towards the changing room I was called back for a second x-ray. As I headed towards the changing room for the second time I was called again for a third x-ray! By that time I knew there was cause for concern. I asked the radiologist if something was wrong. He replied, "Yes! But I cannot discuss it with you." My x-rays were taken to the doctors and nurses that headed the department. I was placed on a bed, and the necessary preparations were done to admit me to the General Hospital.

I remembered hearing a nurse saying, "Why did they take so long to admit this lady?" I knew I was in a critical condition. It all happened so quickly my only comfort was "God was on my side." Being in hospital, I had a chance of receiving proper health care to recover from my illness. Pastor Auguste was in the waiting area wondering why I was delayed. She later was informed that I was admitted to hospital.

◙

5

HOSPITALISED

That Thursday morning I was admitted to the surgical ward, bed number four. It was situated close to a window over-looking the sea which offered me a panoramic view. The boats travelling to Carriacou and Trinidad in addition to the large cargo ships were seen on a regular basis.

When the news concerning my illness and that I was hospitalised began to circulate, everyone was shocked. I remembered a brother who came to visit me one day, looked at me and said "When I heard you were in hospital, I said "I will not believe unless I see for myself!". Family and friends locally and overseas were informed about my illness and prayers were offered up daily for me. As I laid there I thought of the mission trip and recalled talking to a nurse when I was in the emergency room about it. She responded by saying, "You will go on your trip". At that time I felt encouraged, but now what was developing was not looking good. The nurses came around and did their routine pressure checks and vitals. All that time, I had no knowledge of my diagnosis.

Later that day I was accompanied by a nurse to do an ultrasound. While I waited to be attended to I felt nauseous and a kidney dish was given to me. By then I had not eaten for about five days and I had no bowel movement. The ultrasound showed I had a gaseous stomach. After the procedure was completed I was taken back to the ward to await the official results. When I was settled on my bed, I was told I missed a visit from my sister Margaret from the United States. I was a bit disappointed having not seen her for an extended period. Later that afternoon Garvin came by to see me he was very disturbed, close to tears.

Some of the rumours going around included: "I am in the hospital taking my last breath" and these comments had a negative impact on my son. He remained a few minutes at my bedside then left. The doctor passed by that afternoon along with the ward sister and took a look at me, but I was not given any information concerning my illness. Apart from giving birth to my two children in hospital, this was my first time in hospital. The thought of being prepared for surgery was so alien to me, I prayed frequently knowing that only God knew the future and my life was in his hand.

Dinner was served but I could not eat. I lay back as I watched the trolley being pushed carefully arranged with meals for the patients. There were some patients who were recovering from surgeries, while others were awaiting surgeries. They were seated quite comfortably enjoying their dinner. Others were in pain; groaning could have been heard coming from different sections of the Ward. The word of God says *In everything give thanks: for this is the will of God in Christ Jesus concerning you.* – 1 Thes.5:18 KJV. In times of great difficulties it takes faith and trust in God to do so. Lying on that bed I had to cast all my cares upon the Lord and believe him for the best. The day gave way to night and the nurses made their final rounds. The light on the ward went out leaving just the light in the nurses' station. I could not sleep so I lay awake praying that the night will soon turn to dawn. Now and then I glared at the clock to see the time. The night was still, and I could have heard vehicles coming and going from the ward. Intermittently I heard voices calling for the nurse. I might have dozed off briefly; the moment I opened my eyes the nurses were getting ready to begin their usual morning routine.

During that Friday morning a doctor and the ward sister came to give me a nasogastric tube. Inserting it was the most difficult thing I had to do. I pulled it out about twice then I remembered the portion of scripture that says *I can do all things through Christ which strengtheneth me* – Phil. 4:13 KJV. Then I was able to insert the tube. Resting on my bed I overheard a conversation which gave me the motivation to ask the doctor what was my diagnosis. When the doctor passed by that day I said "Doctor what is my diagnosis?" and he replied by saying "I have two bit of news, good news and bad news. The good news is you have gallstones, and the bad news you have Colon Cancer." That was the most devastating news anyone could hear, but strange enough when I heard it I laughed and said, "My God is bigger than Cancer." After the doctor left my bedside, I reasoned with myself along the lines of healing. I saw many people received healing in my ministry but now here I was lying on a hospital bed in need of healing. I knew I could not give up but I had to take God at his word to receive healing. In my conversation with the doctor, he told me he will perform surgery and give me a colostomy bag. At that time I had no idea what that entails and how it would affect my life.

My family knew all along what was the cause of my illness, but they kept quiet, fearing my response to such tragic news. I had a tumour in my colon which prevented me from having bowel movements. That same Friday afternoon the doctor came back to see me and when he looked at the fluid in the nasogastric bag he said, "Not good get her ready for emergency surgery." The nurses hurriedly got me ready and I was wheeled out of the surgical ward into the operating theatre.

This was the first time I experienced being in a theatre. As I looked around me I saw everyone dressed in coats, hats and gloves. I was placed on a narrow bed with my head at a very low level. It was rather uncomfortable. One of the surgeons, after noticing my discomfort elevated my head with a small headrest. A lady in the room told me nicely that she was responsible for giving me the anaesthetic. I was given an injection minutes later and that's all I remembered.

WAKING UP IN THE ICU

I awakened incognisant of the time and day. I knew from my surroundings I was not on the regular ward. Early that morning Pastor Auguste came to see me and told me it was Saturday morning and I was in the Intensive Care Unit (ICU) She prayed for me and by her expression I knew she was holding back tears. It was a brief visit as no one is allowed an extensive stay in the ICU. Only close family were allowed on that ward, special hats and coats were provided before entering the unit. I touched my left side and felt a bulge. I knew then that the colostomy bag was in place, but I was too weak to be concerned about it.

Most things that happened on that day were a blur, but I do remember two nurses took excellent care of me. Even when I was not conscious of my surroundings, prayers were being offed up by the saints of God for me. That Sunday morning my mother and sister Janis came to visit me. When my mother saw my condition she became very emotional and assured me that I will make it, God will see me through.

I was very weak at that time and was in a very critical condition, many people wanted to see me but they had to wait until I returned to the surgical ward. Sister Josephine visited me that Sunday morning and related to me the conversation we held. She told me that I said I can relate to the three Hebrew boys. If the

Lord calls me, I know I did my best for him on earth. She said I also told her that I believe I would make it since there was a lot that I still had to do for God here on planet earth. I instructed her to go back to the brethren at Trinity Hall Ministries and encourage them, and tell Pastor Auguste that I needed to see her, but don't tell her that I had cancer, as I wanted to tell her myself. She prayed a short prayer for me and left. (This is what she related to me).

As a result of my illness I was forced to cancel my mission trip to Barbados. Pastor Kelvin and his congregation were very disappointed that I was unable to be present with them for the appointed time. They were more concerned about the state of my health though and gave the assurance of their prayers for my speedy recovery. Garvin came to see me while I was still in the Intensive Care Unit and he looked very pensive. It was difficult to tell what was going through his mind. Then he spoke up and said "Mom they sent your clothes home, they said you will not have use for them." After a short visit he said goodbye and departed. Following his visit I pondered on what he told me. I knew he was hurting deeply.

The following morning I was asked to get my Pastor to pray for me because I had to be taken to the operating theatre once more. With the help of a nurse, Pastor Auguste was contacted. She immediately responded to the request and on her way to work she came to the ICU. By then my condition had deteriorated. I could tell it was not easy for her to see me in such a helpless condition.

Matthew 18:19 says *Again I say unto you, that if two of you shall agree on earth as touching anything that they shall ask, it shall be done for them of my father which is in heaven.*

She prayed for me and we agreed that morning based on the word of God, though my recovery seemed unlikely through human eyes we knew that all things are possible with God. I also prayed that if I did not survive, I would be with the Lord. I told her my mind was made up.

Whatever the Lord decided to do with me I was satisfied. I had no physical strength so I just surrendered myself to God and asked that his will be done.

After Pastor's departure the doctor and nurse came to attend to me. The nurse attempted on several occasions to draw blood for testing but was unable to locate any veins in my body. After trying without success, she told the doctor she was having difficulty locating my veins. All that time I was praying and pleading with God to help them find a vein. The doctor moved over to my bedside and placed the needle in a horizontal position on my leg and miraculously the blood was drawn. I was very grateful to God for having the blood drawn to facilitate the test and ultimately, the surgery.

I was praying the Twenty Third Psalm over and over in my mind especially the verse that said, *Yea though I walk through the valley of the shadow of death, I will fear no evil.*

If this psalm was a CD, I know it would have been scratched. This song by Kirk Franklyn "I know that I can make it" also became a source of encouragement to me. I was taken back to the operating theatre, but this time my body was showing signs of shutting down.

I remembered saying I was allergic to brown surgical tape and in a flash I drifted into a deep sleep.

◉

6

A GLIMPSE OF GLORY

There is a special programme on television hosted by Sid Roth, called "Its Supernatural." I used to sit imbibed with the stories of near-death experience by various guests. In my heart the near-death experience was phenomenal; the part I did not embrace was the pain and suffering. Lying on the hospital bed I knew it was about to happen to me, there was a transition taking place in my body that I did not understand neither did I have the power to control it. The white ceiling over my head was no longer in view – instead my body took its place. I could have seen the veins and blood flowing through my body. I knew I was leaving this world because my thoughts were no longer earthly, something stronger than my will was steering me into a new dimension. I then found myself in a large place where everything was orange in colour and the presence of God was felt in a dynamic way. The only person present with me was Garth, the son of Sister Josephine. I saw no one else in that place. When he felt the power of God he said, "Now I believe." I was drifting in and out of consciousness and found myself standing close to the door, as I turned back I saw my body lying on the bed. No one was in view so I immediately left the room and I ended up in a place I was not familiar with. The first thing I recognised there was a sign with a blue light shaped like an arrow pointing up. In another place I saw a tunnel and I started advancing towards it, but I was distracted. I opened my eyes to find a nurse at my bedside. They knew I was leaving but they were doing all in their power to keep me alive. Moments later I was in this awesome place, and this time I found myself in the company of multitudes of coloured people all dressed in white robes. I knew instantly I was in heaven in the company of God's people. I was sitting among them and for the first time, understood what it really meant to be carefree. It was a good place to be: no pain, no tears, no sorrow and no thoughts of earth. I was in silence for the whole time, in my state of euphoria a stout lady whom I cannot say that I had seen before, lifted her head and looked me straight in the eyes and said, "What are you doing here?" I replied, "That is what I want to find out." Then I realised I should not be there and I started withdrawing myself. I then had an encounter with angels, I saw their robes – I beheld the exquisite glow of whiteness. It appeared as if light was emitting from those robes. It was a magnificent sight far beyond earthly explanation! I knew they were coming to take me away; as they were approaching me I shouted *I shall not die but live and declare the works of the Lord* – Psalm 118:17 KJV. The angels quickly departed from me.

The Bible says *the word of God is quick and powerful and sharper than any two-edged sword –* Heb: 4:12 KJV. If we have faith in God's word it will work for us in our times of difficulties. Physically I felt helpless and was surrendering to death, but my spirit-man knew it was not my time to die. It is imperative that believers read their Bibles and pray often. These are savings account to be utilised when necessary. I was able to withdraw from my word account to save my life.

On my way back I was detained by an evil stone with eyes. I found myself in a basement and there was this stone about 31cm long and 51cm in circumference, the colour was black and its orange eyes were evident. It appeared to be just an ordinary stone but it had immense power to kill and destroy. I know my God is the head of all principalities and power (Col 2:10 KJV) so when I realised I was not capable of fighting this battle on my own, I cried out saying "Lord, send back-up!" Suddenly, I heard loud singing and praying coming from the church. They were in deep spiritual warfare. The stone was not about to surrender without a fight; It continued to throw dirt on me the objective was to kill me. I was fully aware that this was spiritual wickedness in high places. I fought back as hard as I could; the church continued to sing and pray, but the stone kept throwing dirt on me. As the battle intensified it appeared as if the stone would succeed in trying to bury me alive; it was now life or death. As the stone was about to throw the final set of dirt on me to cover me; the church landed a knockout blow and I opened my eyes on the bed for a brief moment. In glance flash a doctor was by my bedside and I was on life support.

That's all I remembered. I might have slipped back into unconsciousness. I later opened my eyes and was thirsty to the point of dehydration. In a very weak voice I said "wa-ter, wa-ter." The nurse responded by saying, "you cannot drink water." However, she cracked an ice cube and placed tiny bits on my lips. It was not much but it helped. I was taken off life-support but remained relatively weak.

I am a firm believer in the Bible. I believe it is the inspired word of God. I always thought of heaven before I got sick. I can recall at times I would look up to the sky and say, "I wonder what is happening in heaven now?" I now have proof that there is life after death and that heaven is real.

The doctor passed on the Tuesday morning, assessed my condition and said to the nurses: "We have done all we can, put her down on the surgical ward." When I heard that statement I knew exactly what it meant. Any further help for me must come from God and it must be a miracle. The nurses got me ready and the orderly came in and wheeled me back to the surgical ward.

◉

7

RETURN TO SURGICAL WARD

I was back on bed number four close to the window again, hooked up to oxygen and intravenous rehydration tubes. Family and friends now had the opportunity to visit me. I was in a better position to process information about my surgery. I was told a large tumour was removed from my colon and two lymph nodes were affected. My surgery was a laparotomy and a major one.

The following morning when the team of doctors checked in on me, they examined the incision and determined that part of it showed signs of infection. The nurses were ordered to remove fourteen stitches. This procedure left a large opening in my abdomen. I thought I would have to return to the theatre to close up that space but that was not the case. The nurses dressed me daily covering the area with gauze and surgical tape. I had difficulties breathing. Whenever I was told by the doctor to take a big breath, as hard as I tried I could not get it done. As a result of this, I was afraid to fall asleep because I often felt as if my head was leaving the bed and I was about to die. After repeated efforts and lung exercise with no sign of improvement, blood samples were taken and sent to Saint Augustine's Hospital for testing. Later that day the results came back showing that I had blood clots in my lungs. I was immediately given a prescribed drug Warfarin which helped to thin the blood. The dietician came by that same week with information on the foods I should eat and those I should abstain from. My condition that time was critical but stable. Bren, after hearing of my illness sought permission to visit me. That morning when he walked in he was escorted by prison officials.

When he saw me he had an expression of sadness on his face. His father died when he was very young, and I could tell by the look on his face he was afraid of losing his only parent. After a short visit it was time for him to leave, my eyes followed as they left my bedside. I had many visitors. Most of them were Christian brethren. Pastor Auguste visited regularly. Sister Josephine who was very concerned about me, called often to find out about my progress, and made it her duty to visit. Pastor Hyacinth and her family were very supportive to me while in hospital. The first Sunday after my return to the Ward, she came and prayed for me, and while she was praying my body began to sweat profusely. I knew at that time the power of God was touching my body.

The following morning sister Nicolet was sent by God with a message of hope for me. She said "The Lord says it is well" As she spoke, her body shook under the anointing I was encouraged by her message and from then on I was even more motivated to trust God for my full recovery.

One morning I wanted to use the bedpan but I was unable to get up on my own. A patient who normally walked around and help other patients that needed assistance, helped me to get on the bedpan. When I was finished there wasn't anyone close by to help me, so I tried to get off on my own and instantly I felt a sharp pain, then my bladder was unable to contain the urine. It resulted in me having to wear disposable diapers. Before my illness I never imagined that one day I would be wearing disposable diapers, there I was lying in bed like a baby. Many people had given up hope on me recovering, including some doctors and nurses, but I had faith and I knew the Lord would see me through. I refused to accept defeat.

I had a great desire to hear the word of God, and to listen to worship songs, but I was too weak to read my Bible. I depended on others to read to me. I can recall one night I wanted someone to read to me. I saw one of the hospital staff and I asked her if she can read to me, she answered by saying she forgot her glasses at home. I was very disappointed that night, however, a doctor on the ward had a phone with gospel music and she left it with me for a while. I was refreshed and inspired listening to those songs, it was such a blessing although I was too weak to sing but in my heart I felt the peace of God. The following night a thirteen year old patient on a bed next to me took the initiative to read to me and explain the Scriptures. On Sundays there was a constant flow of visitors to the hospital. They came from different denominations to pray and encourage the sick. On this particular occasion a middle aged man, partly sober passed by my bed and spoke words of comfort to me. I was encouraged by the words he spoke. That encounter made me realise that God can use anybody to carry out his will even a drunk!

As the difficulties to sleep persisted I would lay wide awake frequently staring at the clock. This pattern continued for quite a while until I started hearing voices coming from a corner of the ward at night. When I turned my attention to the corner where the sounds were coming from no one was there. I knew too well if I did not get to sleep at once, I was heading for a nervous breakdown.

Without further hesitation I requested prayer from some Christian friends and that same night I slept. My sleeping improved but was plagued with scary dreams and speaking out loudly in my sleep. One night in a dream I heard myself speaking loudly, immediately I woke up and the nurse who always worked night shift on that ward was standing close to my bed. I turned my head in her direction and said: "I had a dream" I didn't want anyone to think that I was mentally challenged.

One morning that same nurse said to me "A young woman like you, you lie down there in pampers." Her remarks pierced me like an arrow. I don't know whether she was trying to help me and didn't know how to phrase her sentence politely or whether she was trying to intimidate me. I remembered praying and crying before God to help me get out of the hospital. What she said gave me the motivation to push myself to regain strength and to get out of disposable diapers. Everyone loves to be spoken to gently and with love but sometimes it takes harsh words to get us out of our comfort zone. I later spoke to the nurse and thanked her. The beds in the hospital are very high unlike regular beds. The thought of going down the bed always brought fear to me.

One Sunday morning I called a nurse and asked her to show me how to get off the bed. She was very kind and she explained to me how to get it done. I dressed myself that Sunday in a beautiful nightgown. It was a difficult task to get off that bed, but I held on to the rails and I slowly made my way down. When my feet touched the floor they felt heavy and numb. I held unto the bedside chair and eased myself down until I was safely seated. I remained there for a few minutes then slowly made my way back unto the bed. The following day I went down the bed again and holding unto the railing I walked around the bed. The third day I took a few steps and looked in the second section of the ward which consisted of four sections. I knew I was making progress! The fourth day I got down the bed and walked to the third section and entered the wash room. When I looked into the mirror I almost did not recognise myself, I had lost over twenty pounds. One Friday morning two wonderful Christian friends brought a vase of flowers along with other items and decorated my bed side table beautifully; I was also given a make-up bag filled with make-up. I was very excited. I applied some make up and sat on the bedside chair. Some of the nurses complimented me because they saw how eager and hard I was working to look and feel better. The days that followed I worked on training my bladder.

After a few days I was out of disposable diapers. My appetite was now perfect. I never for one moment was worried about the cancer. In fact, every day I looked forward with anticipation to hear the heavy trolley that carried the meals. The lighter trolley was the medication and I was not thrilled about that one, because most times I got injections. I was recovering and the doctors and nurses commented on how well I was doing. I was now trained by the nurses to change my colostomy bag. I was gradually learning to cope but not without challenges. On one occasion I woke up in the night; the bag was detached and my clothing was soiled. There was a small opening in the neck of the night gown, so I used a pair of scissors to cut it straight down the front to free myself.

The end of November 2011 was fast approaching and I wondered whether I would be in hospital for Christmas. I still had visitors on a daily basis and many of them were very generous. Some of them read the Bible and sang for me. I love singing very much but on those occasions I was unable to participate. As the days followed I was taken off the oxygen and the intravenous rehydration (drips). The morning of November 29, the team of doctors on their routine checks after reviewing my records with smiles and words of encouragement signed my discharge papers. I was now free to go home; I felt very excited after prolonged illness and uncertainty that the hour had finally come.

Garvin was informed and by the time he arrived at the hospital I was already dressed and ready to go. All my belongings were taken to the entrance of the hospital. I said good bye to the patients and nurses and slowly made my way to the car which was parked at the entrance. I carefully got into the front seat and placed a pillow on my lap to mitigate the effects on my body from the bumps in the road. Garvin drove cautiously as we made our way home.

◉

8

CHALLENGES FACED

I was taken back to Allen's home until I was capable of handling things on my own. The family did their best in caring for me, and made me quite comfortable. Sister Harriet also took time from her busy schedule and assisted the family with my laundry. Being out of the hospital I was now fully aware that I had a disability. I had to make a number of adjustments in order to accommodate the colostomy bag. I am not an ostentatious person but I always believe a minister should be properly dressed. However, with the bag on my side I resorted to loose clothing. My high heel shoes were abandoned and I had to settle for flats and slippers on a daily basis. For one month daily, I woke up very early and made my way to the clinic to have the incision attended to. I also took weekly blood tests to monitor the warfarin.

One morning after dressing at the clinic, I was outside waiting for my son to pick me up. In the distance I saw a man approaching. I felt lead to speak to him, so I said good morning and started a conversation with him. My encounter with this man was not a coincidence. I was surprised to learn that he was also living with a colostomy. He even showed me his side where it was attached. After speaking to him, I felt quite encouraged. I said to myself "I am not an isolated case, there were other people facing the same challenges as me. I will make it."

Before I became ill, my whole life was centered on the ministry. I went out of my way to help many people and in turn some of them gave their full support to me in whatever way they could. I was unable to do very much at that time and sometimes I became very depressed especially looking at my body with the bag and scars. The colostomy had its fair share of challenges. It was new to me and I had to do research to find out as much as I could. I had to be very careful when leaving home; always ensuring the bag was properly secured by putting a layer of white surgical tape around the adhesive just to be safe. The bags were very expensive and there were times when my supply ran low I had to limit the places I went in order to conserve bags.

A few weeks after my release from hospital, I was introduced to someone who had been living with a colostomy for many years. She came to my rescue on several occasions by giving me colostomy bags. She was someone I called on while learning to cope with my challenges. Whenever I contemplated going out, I avoided eating peas, beans and breadfruit to prevent the release of extra gas into the bag which could cause a balloon effect under my garment.

By speaking to people I received information of other people living with colostomy. It was very comforting when I contacted some of them and we were able to share our experiences. Two weeks after my discharge from the hospital I was due to attend the out-patient clinic. That morning I arrived very early, yet there were a number of people already there. I took a seat on one of the benches provided. I waited about two hours before the medical team arrived. I spotted my surgeon and I called out to him but there was no response. Different specialists operate in that section of the hospital so many people were waiting to see their doctors that day.

I was sitting with the cancer patients and I made conversation with those close to me. Some of their stories were rather interesting. Some cancer survivors also came and introduced themselves to us and shared their testimonies. One that really stood out in my mind was a lady that celebrated five years as a survivor. With treatment and her faith in God she received her healing and became cancer free. She spoke to us with great conviction, I was encouraged on that day and I knew that my total recovery was dependent on my faith. The doctors commenced attendance and slowly the benches were becoming less populated. My name was called and I made my way to the doctor's office. My surgeon's assistant was present looking at my results and verifying the reports. When my surgeon walked in he was surprised to see me doing so well. I said "Doctor, I called you when you were entering." He replied, "I was looking to see a sick woman." The effects of the cancer were still evident in parts of my body but I knew I was slowly recovering with God's help. The weekly blood tests and the warfarin had to be continued and I was referred to the oncologist by my doctor. After my first visit to the oncologist I was sent to do a Computed Tomography Scan (CT Scan). The results were not so favourable but I did not allow that to discourage me from my firm belief, that God will heal me from cancer.

On a date appointed I was called in by the Oncology Department. The nurse's role was to explain to me how the chemotherapy works and the side effects I should expect. To me it sounded like a fifty-fifty chance of survival. I was given a file with reading material to take home. The nurse was very convincing based on her experience having survived cancer herself. The following week I was scheduled to commence the chemotherapy, but first I had to meet with the oncologist and his team. I got home that day with my mind in turmoil. I had a decision to make: chemotherapy or no chemotherapy? After giving it much thought I still was not certain what to do, I decided to seek God's guidance. After praying I lay on my bed and I had a vision. I saw myself on a bed at the point of death, and this was the result of taking chemotherapy. When I came out of that vision I made up my mind to refuse the chemo but to trust the Lord for healing.

Many people including family members urged me to take the treatment but I told them no because I knew If I took it I would not survive. **I wish to state categorically that I am not discouraging any cancer patient from taking treatment as recommended by their physicians. I am only sharing my experience.**

By April 2012, I was anxious to get the colostomy reversed. It was five months since I was living with this: I was scorned by some people and rejected by others. Disparaging remarks which I rather not to mention were cast at me. Sometimes I would just weep before God and ask Him "how long this will continue?" I made an appointment that month and went to see my surgeon. He told me I had to do a few tests one of which was the Barium Enema. This is a procedure where there's a machine set up, a liquid is sent through the colostomy (stoma) via a tube and pictures are taken. The same procedure was done through the rectum and the photos were taken of the organs inside. It was an uncomfortable procedure which I hope I never have to repeat.

A few days later the results were available in the form of a CD and a written report. I knew it was the grace of God that kept me strong and positive because the truth is, the results were not satisfactory.

When I went for my doctor's appointment I knew he was not happy with the results, when I questioned him about my chances of reversal he told me during surgery he will see and decide what to do. It was now time for me to return to the oncologist with the results.

That morning my son dropped me off at the hospital, but I didn't think it was necessary for him to accompany me, so I went to the doctor's office alone. Days prior to my appointment I felt deeply troubled in my spirit. When my name was called and I opened the door leading to the doctor's office, I knew why I felt the way I did. The medical team awaiting me was comprised of three, I was asked whether I came alone to which I answered: "yes" then I handed the CT scan to the oncologist. He closely examined the results which showed that there was still evidence of cancer in my body. The minutes that followed he encouraged me to consider the chemotherapy treatment. I listened in silence then finally spoke and said adamantly, "I am not taking the chemo." Astonishment was on the faces of the three that comprised the medical team. I was asked, why and although my legs were still painful I mustered up all the strength and courage and said: "I am healed." I was told many people said that before and ended up dying. I surely didn't want to die. I sat there for a moment pondering on what was said. Not having anyone with me to discuss the matter I had to think for myself. A scripture came to my mind and I said, *"For me to live is Christ and to die is gain"* – Phil 1:21 KJV. Silence followed my statement. However, when they spoke words of encouragement and support were expressed. I was assured that the final decision was mine.

When I arrived home that day as I lay on my bed, I began to think of the humungous decision that I made only hours before; something I had to defend with my faith. There was now no turning back. Later that day I called my close family and friends and informed them of my decision. My sister strongly recommended that I take at least two cycles of the chemo. She even came up with a strategic plan to raise funds for the treatment. I told her unequivocally I was not taking the treatment. She could not understand why I was bent on rejecting the chemo, but I knew I was doing the right thing. Six months after my surgery I relocated to my home in Independence Avenue with my son Garvin.

My surgery was scheduled for June 2012. I wanted to be optimistic that the colostomy would be reversed, but in my heart there were negative niggling thoughts. The day before my surgery I had a little talk with myself, it was a "what if" discussion. I said what if when I wake up from surgery the bag is still attached to my side, what will I do then? I answered my own question by saying, "I will continue my life as I did before the surgery."

My children were very happy for me. My mom told me using the bags posed too many challenges. They all thought I would finally get my life back. All arrangements were made and I was only awaiting the date for my admission to the hospital.

◉

9

IT TOOK A MIRACLE

The morning had finally come; I arrived in the hospital before eight o'clock. I was admitted and this time I was in the second section. I had four days to prepare for surgery. This was my third time going to the theatre and I felt a sense of incertitude mixed with anxiety.

I had no pain so I was free to socialise with some of the patients. My surgery took place on a Monday morning. I was back in the theatre and my life was now in the hands of the Lord whom I trusted to work through the medical team. I had faith that everything was going to be fine because prior to the date of my surgery; I had a vision where I saw my abdomen open and looking clean and healthy. The anaesthetic was administered, and I drifted off to sleep. I was awakened by a nurse in the recovery room and when I felt my side the colostomy bag was still there. I said "Nurse the bag is still with me" and she replied "The doctor will talk to you." I was disappointed but yet encouraged, because I felt negative before the surgery and I had made up my mind whatever the outcome I will continue to trust in the Lord. I was taken back to the ward and placed in the first section near to the window on bed four.

My family and friends were disappointed. My children felt sorry for me wondering if I will have to live out my life with a disability. Some of the patients whom I got acquainted with were sorry that things did turn out as expected. When the doctor passed he told me since I did not have chemotherapy he was not sure if reversing at that time was the right thing to do. However, a sample of the colon was sent for testing. I spent just a few days in hospital and was released. A few weeks after my release from hospital, I went to see my surgeon and when he saw me entering the door to his office he said, "I have some good news for you, the cancer did not return." I was so excited, that I went to the lab immediately and got the official results.

I am thankful to God every day for his miraculous healing. Life has more meaning to me now than prior to my illness. There were things I took for granted and there were times I knew I could have been more grateful for God's blessings. I try on a daily basis to maintain a strict diet including drinking lots of water and using fresh fruits. I will not allow the good report to cause me to become complacent. I enjoyed different types of food before that were not in keeping with a healthy lifestyle but I gave them all up and I don't miss them. In August, two months after my surgery, one Sunday was designated as "National Day of Prayer" in Grenada. That morning as I approached the building where our services were usually held along with other members, I saw something that almost brought tears to my eyes. Another church was occupying our space. I saw ushers at the doorway and I began interrogating them hoping to find some answers, but no one was willing to tell me the truth. When we left the premises that morning, I remembered a dream I had months before and in that dream I went to church one Sunday morning and none of our members was present; instead there were people that I did not know.

The following Monday I made an inquiry and I was told they were informed that I was sick so they gave the building to another church. This was done without a verbal or written notice which resulted in total embarrassment to the Ministry. We then attended the church of another Pastor for a short while. After seeking help from someone I knew, we were allowed to use another building – but by then some of the members had lost interest and had stopped attending church. Having informed some of the members that I would come with a bus to pick them up one Sunday morning, I became very discouraged when I got there. I waited patiently but no one turned up. I called and was told that they would not be attending church. That Sunday Pastor Auguste had another engagement so I had no form of support. I was still recovering and the stress of the ministry was becoming unbearable. The ministry was my life, that was all I looked forward to, but I had a choice either to continue struggling with the church and die or give up and live. After speaking to a dear friend I was advised to release the members. It was not easy to make those phone calls but I had to. After much prayer and tears I called everyone and told them they were released from the ministry and that they were free to attend a church according to the Lord's leading.

It took me months to come to terms with what transpired, and to begin attending a church close to me. I know God is in control and He has a plan for my life and in due season it will come to pass. I know Trinity Hall Ministries will rise again based on what was revealed to me and confirmed by a prophet in the USA. From my experience as a minister I can say to believers, "If you are not called of God to get involved in ministry, be content to sit on the pews." Being in ministry requires tenacity and strong faith. We have to remember Jesus and the twelve disciples he chose. He taught them, fed them, they even saw him cry. When the time came for Jesus to die a painful death, He was forsaken. That was when he needed his friends the most. I was doing a very good job pasturing a church. However, my calling was on the mission field. In other words I was not in the will of God. Two months after I decided to do what the Lord told me to do, I almost lost my life to cancer.

As believers we must always make sure we are doing the will of God. Man may ordain us and give us titles but we will have no peace of mind until we are operating in the will of God. I thank God for all he has brought me through I am now a stronger person, gold must enter the fire to be tested. When I was a young Christian I told the Lord I wanted to be an extraordinary Christian. I was naive at that time, but I can boldly say now we have to be careful with the statements we make because death and life are in the power of the tongue and we will get what we ask for. The year was far advancing coming to a close and

I still had in my possession a one year ticket bearing an expiry date of November 2012. I considered my options and decided not to let that money go to waste, I contacted my host Pastor Kelvin in Barbados and made arrangements to travel in October. It was a test of my strength because I was recovering from surgery and was still using the colostomy bag.

The days that followed I studied and prepared myself for a one-week crusade in which I was the featured speaker. It was a major challenge for me but I stood on the word which says *I can do all things through Christ which strengtheneth me* Phil: 4:13-KJV. I did all my packing which included one month supply of colostomy bags. I made a visit to my doctor informing him of my travel arrangements. He gave me some medical advice and told me on my return we would discuss the reversal surgery.

10

MY MISSION TRIP

When I arrived at Maurice Bishop International Airport that Saturday afternoon, I checked with the airline at the counter. It was early for my flight, so I walked around and visited a couple stores and purchased a few items. There was a smooth flow of traffic as passengers were seen carrying suitcases making their way to the check-in counters. It was then time for me to go through immigration. My bags and shoes went through the scanner and as I was going through, a female security officer approached me and started giving me a pat down.

I knew I was wearing my colostomy bag, so before she got to that area I quickly informed her about the bag. She questioned what it was, and I replied it was a medical device. I offered to show her and she agreed to have a look. I followed her to what was supposed to be an opened room but unfortunately the door was locked. So I stood in front of the door and showed her the bag. When she saw it she became very sympathetic and asked: "Are you alright?" and I replied "yes." I then proceeded to the counter, retrieved my belongings and sat in the departure lounge.

The flight was delayed so I contacted Pastor Phillips to inform him. As I sat there I had some overwhelming thoughts – recalling the times when I was so weak that I was unable to walk without the support of someone. I pondered on the goodness of God and where he had taken me from, because I was now travelling alone.

The airport was relatively slow, not much activity was taking place. After what should be deemed as a lengthy wait, from my vantage point the LIAT plane was touched down at MBIA. Simultaneously I heard the announcements asking passengers to prepare for boarding. I got my bags together and advanced to the check-out counter. In minutes I was on my way along with other passengers to board the plane. After about forty-five minutes of flying, we landed at Grantley Adams International Airport safely.

It was a busy day at the airport but the immigration lines were moving swiftly, and within minutes my check was completed. I briskly walked to the luggage area and collected my suitcase and I exited the building. On the outside, many people were anxiously awaiting their love ones, while others were seen holding placards as a form of identification. I had no difficulty locating Pastor Phillips. At one glance I saw him and he came forward and warmly welcomed me.

A lot had changed in Barbados since my last visit three years prior to this one. I noticed enormous development had taken place. We headed to St. Thomas, where I stayed during my one month visit. On my arrival there, I was greeted by a wonderful couple who owned the apartment where I was housed. It was a beautifully decorated apartment, I immediately felt at home. I was informed by Pastor Phillips that the crusade was brought forward by one week due to various extenuating circumstances. That meant I only had one week to conclude my preparation.

Life as we know it is very unpredictable. Sometimes we have lots of plans, but we never know how they will actually play out. In spite of the outcome, I have learned never to feel sorry for myself because that can only lead to depression or distorted thinking. As the scripture says in Prov. 23:7 KJV *As a man thinketh in his heart so is he*. We follow our thoughts. Hence it is important that we have positive ones. I knew I could not give up on my ministry because of a disability. I often told people as long as I can speak I will be sharing my testimony.

The countdown was on for the crusade; all the necessary structures were put in place to ensure a successful week of meetings. Flyers were out and invitations were sent out to various churches. My first Sunday morning at church was a delightful one. I met Pastor's family and the members of his Assembly, who all welcomed me warmly. After service arriving home, I had my lunch and took a rest; knowing in a matter of hours I had to be on my way to the church to preach at the Crusade. This was the first time after my illness, I was invited to preach in a major setting. Some of my close associates were very concerned about me taking on such a challenge in my recovery stage; but what the Lord had done for me was miraculous and I could not keep it quiet. I had faith that the crusade would be successful. The service was scheduled for 7pm.

When I arrived that night at the church, the worship leaders were about to take their place at the altar to begin the night service. Many people heard of my cancer survival and they came out to hear and see what God had done. The singing and worship were heard resonating throughout the community as the musicians played skillfully and the worshippers sang lustily all for the honour and glory of God.

Then it was time for the pastor to welcome me to the podium. It was a momentous occasion for me to be able to share my testimony and expound the word of God. As a result of my sharing, many were blessed and had their faith in God strengthened. During the crusade the Lord performed miracles of healing among his people. One lady, who was suffering with rheumatoid arthritis, was healed during a service while sitting in the congregation; she believed and the power of God was present to heal her. There were many other reported cases of healing which took place. Some people surrendered to Jesus while others received deliverance from demonic spirits, and were baptized by the Holy Spirit with the evidence of speaking in tongues. Approaching the culmination of the crusade, the building was filled to capacity. The word was spread of the working of the hand of God. It was a great revival for everyone who attended the crusade.

Following the crusade, I attended a week of meetings with Pastor Phillips and family at

Mount Zion's Missions Int'l; I was welcomed by the church and was given the opportunity to share my testimony and a brief exhortation. The following week I had another opportunity to minster at a church in St. Andrew. We had a great time in the presence of the Lord and many sick people received healing. My host Pastor made arrangements for me to share my testimony on radio and in the print media. I went shopping a few times accompanied by good friends. I truly felt loved and appreciated among God's people. This would not have been made possible without the assistance of Pastor Phillips. The courtesy extended to me by him and his family was awesome. As I was preparing to return home, my thoughts were focused on my incomplete journey. I had to make preparations for another surgery.

A few days before my return to Grenada I made a call to the airline to confirm my flight back home. I was given an early morning flight. Pastor Phillips dropped me off at the airport and his wife Minister Phillips remained with me to see me off. However, when I got to the counter I was told my name was not in the system. I told the attending clerk that was impossible since I was holding my departure slip. They began checking and rechecking. While I stood there looking at them I said to Minister Phillips: "let us pray" and she agreed. Suddenly the attendant said "I see your name; your flight is scheduled for tonight." I was further advised that I could check-in but I would have to take my luggage with me and check it in later. We called Pastor Phillips who came and took me back to the apartment in St. Thomas. I remained there until it was time to return to the airport.

In the evening when I went back to the airport I had no further difficulties. I had a pleasant flight and landed in Grenada safely. It was good to be back home. When I heard the Grenadian voices on the airport, I said "Thank God I am home."

◉

11

PREPARATION FOR
FINAL SURGERY

One week after my return I had an appointment with my doctor. On that day he told me I would have to carry out a few tests just to make sure everything was in order. It was already late November so my surgery had to be scheduled for 2013. I had some time to prepare so I diverted my attention to Christmas which was the following month. Bren was released from incarceration for the Christmas holidays.

Preparations for Christmas begin in Grenada in November. On the radio and television one can hear and see lots of advertisements, Christmas songs, and carols. In the city some of the stores had speaker boxes at their entrance, with Christmas music being played. The feeling of Christmas was already in the air. This is the time of the year when everyone looks forward with great joy and anticipation. As December approached, Grenadians living overseas would return home for Christmas. Shoppers would be in the city frequently purchasing items to decorate their homes. Black cake (Christmas Fruit Cake), ginger beer, sorrel and pickled ham (salted ham) all form part of our Christmas tradition. When I was a child I didn't understand the meaning of Christmas and all I looked forward to was the food and gifts. When I became a believer, I then understood that Christ came into the world to save me from my sins, and it should be a time of thanksgiving and praise to God for giving us this great gift of his son. I also believe it's a time to remember the less fortunate to bring some joy to their hearts.

By Christmas Eve everyone would have bought their necessities and large crowds of people would converge in the city up to late night eating, drinking, enjoying themselves and purchasing last minute gifts and goodies.

On Christmas morning some churches usually have service at 5am to enable the congregations to spend the day with their families. Oftentimes a steelband would pass early and serenade by playing Christmas Carols. The favourite is usually "We wish you a Merry Christmas." My Christmas was a relatively quiet one. I was thankful to be alive to see another year. Immediately after Christmas I began working on the tests, some of which were rather expensive. The church community along with good friends were very instrumental in providing funds to assist me. By March of 2013 I completed the tests, and this time the results were favourable. My surgery was scheduled for May. This time I felt quite confident that the colostomy would be reversed. Around that same period there was a shortage of colostomy bags. The importer was experiencing serious difficulties in sourcing them. For all of us with colostomy it was rather frustrating. Thanks to my friend who usually assisted me when I ran out of supplies I was able to make it through. A shipment of bags arrived in time for my surgery. I was now relieved and packed my bag for the hospital.

The day had finally arrived. It was a Saturday morning when I was transported to the hospital by Pastor Auguste. By 8am I checked in at the nurses' desk and was admitted. When all the paperwork was completed I was shown to my bed which happened to be bed four by the window overlooking the sea. I remembered joking over bed number four as being my bed. My surgery was scheduled for the Monday morning. I kept in constant prayer to maintain a positive mind. I was then living with the colostomy bag for sixteen months and I wanted a normal life again.

Many believers were praying for me because they knew how difficult it was to be going in and out of hospital. I thank God every day for the volume of prayers that went up for me by the Church and the prayer results were tremendous. At times when some of them meet me on the streets, they will look at me in amazement. God is a miracle working God and nothing is impossible with him. Lazarus was dead in the grave for four days and Jesus brought him back to life – John 11:42-44 KJV. It is because of weak faith miracles are not as prevalent as before. All the necessary preparations were made and I was now prepared for surgery. I was wheeled into the theatre and minutes later I was given the anaesthetic.

COLOSTOMY REVERSED

I was awakened hours later in the recovery room with a nurse by my bed side. She said to me the colostomy is reversed do you want to see? I was still very sleepy and I cannot recall what my response was. Minutes later she told me they were taking me back to the surgical ward. I got to the ward and fell asleep again. Sometime during the night I got up! Indeed the bag was gone! I was very excited in my heart but could not show emotions at my recovery stage.

I had some concerns because of the research I did on other patients with colostomy reversal. Some cases were successful and others were not. I remembered reading of one man who after getting a reversal, he had an infection and had to go back to surgery and the bag was reintroduced to him. He had to wait a long time before the procedure was repeated, but at that time it was successful. I wondered whether the colon would move my bowel frequently. I was preoccupied with many thoughts. The third day after my surgery I had very acute diarrhoea which lasted for almost one week. Several tests were done, the appropriate medication was prescribed and two days after taking the drugs I recovered.

Then came Mothers' Day and I was pleasantly surprised when I received a beautiful bouquet of flowers from three of my dear friends. Being in hospital and presented with flowers meant the world to me I felt very elated and thankful. Nine days after my surgery I was discharged from the hospital. I was ecstatic to return to my family, especially knowing that the surgery was successful. I felt as the happiest person on the planet. On my arrival home a sister from our church volunteered to do my laundry and prepare my

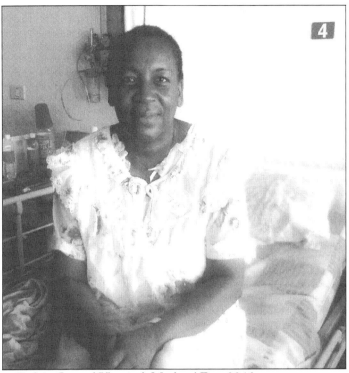

Bed 4, General Hospital. Mothers' Day 2013.

meals. This was answered prayer; God has been so good to me in my times of need. He always provided. I was thankful to God for giving me my life back. The surgeon and his team had done a marvelous job. Day by day I was becoming more confident as my bowel movements normalised. I no longer had to bear the heavy cost of the colostomy bags. It was a delight to be able to wear my normal clothing.

Looking back at all that I suffered it took me back to the book of 1 Samuel Chapter 2:6 KJV with Hannah's song of praise *The Lord killeth, and maketh alive: He bringeth down to the grave, and bringeth up.* While I was in hospital Bren travelled to a neighbouring Island. In July of 2013 Garvin got married it was an experience of a life time to be the mother of the groom. To stand there and actually see my son walking down the aisle with his bride Juliet, stepping into his new life. I had mixed feelings at one point I felt like crying but I fought back the tears. This is a time every parent has to look forward to knowing that one day the children will be grown and will have to leave home.

Faith can move mountains it does not matter what you are going through at this time. Your heart might be broken or you may be diagnosed with cancer or some non-communicable terminal disease. Prov. 18:21 says *death and life are in the power of the tongue.* If you are sick and you choose to speak death over your life you will eventually die. *Faith is the substance of things hoped for the evidence of things not seen* – Heb. 11:1 KJV. Even while believing you may still have the symptoms of your illness, but you have to continue to confess that *you shall not die but live and declare the works of the Lord* – Psalm 118:17 KJV.

We are all on this earth for a purpose. Once we can identify what it is, we have to work towards fulfilling it. It may not be easy but our motto should be "never give up." Even when we feel uncertain of what our purpose is, we know that God has a purpose for us and as long as we walk in his will we will fulfill his purpose in our lives. There would be many challenges, they may come on gradually then become a tempest. I have learnt to trust in the Lord because I know that I cannot make it on my own. There were times in my life when trials came like winds blowing from every direction; tears were then my language which God understood.

Every day of my life when I look in the mirror I see a miracle looking back at me, and I know that God is real, the scripture says, *for the Lord God is a sun and shield: no good thing will he withhold from them that walk uprightly* – Psalm 84:11 KJV.

I enjoy going to the beach. It is refreshing and acts like a therapy, lying on the sand and viewing the horizon while the raging waves lash against the steaming rocks with cruel vengeance. Though I was told it was alright to bathe on the beach with the bag. I refrained from doing so for almost two years. My big day came. One bright sunny afternoon my daughter-in-law Juliet, and I went to the famous Grand Anse Beach. When I arrived I lifted my voice and began to praise God, it was so awesome to enter what I usually refer to as "Papa God's bath tub." The vastness of the waters with its beautiful blue colour enticed me to step in. Without any hesitation I plunged in and oh! How rejuvenated I felt. It was indeed a splendid afternoon; Juliet and I had great fun.

What was rather interesting was I met some of my primary schoolmates on the beach. They had come home on vacation from the USA and Canada. Imagine not seeing friends for over forty years! that was a lot of catching up to do.

To those of you, who will read my experience, if you are living with a colostomy bag that is irreversible, don't be discouraged, it will take time and patience but trust in the Lord and pray. I know of a lady living with a colostomy for over twelve years. She travels and lives a normal life, I have never seen her sad. If you are out there waiting on reversal, when the doctor is satisfied with all your test results your surgery will be done.

A few months following the reversal of my colostomy I experience some minor difficulties with bowel movements as a result of consuming too many peanuts. Prior to that I was talking with someone who had advised me to be careful, and had also told me of someone who had to undergo surgery for blockage in the colonic area. There is an old saying "A word to the wise is sufficient." From that time I consumed peanuts occasionally to avoid the negative impact on my body. I did research on Aloe and found out about its medicinal properties: curing constipation headed the list. I thought it would be a good idea to use a little. I started using a little. I would peel off the skin, drain the latex (yellow liquid) and eat the gel. One day I decided to blend some. I was in a hurry that morning. After picking the aloe in my garden I didn't allow it to drain properly. After blending it I noticed that it was unusually bitter. I gave my son some to taste and he told me it was too bitter. However, I placed it on the refrigerator and two days later forgetting how bitter it was I poured a glass and drank most of it. The following day I started developing some discomfort in my stomach and this lasted for about a week. When I recovered I made a promise to myself to be extra careful even when in a hurry.

I continued to seek the Lord for complete healing. Psalm 139.16 KJV speaks of our body parts written in God's book. I often prayed that scripture for a new colon having lost most of my descending colon. The third anniversary of my illness was November 2014 when that time was approaching I noticed I was having discomfort in my stomach and problems with bowel movements. The first week I prayed and limited my diet to one meal a day. I couldn't sit for long periods. I only felt comfortable standing or lying down. The second week the problem worsened. I kept my feelings to myself because I didn't want my family to worry and I definitely resented the thought of returning to hospital. I continued my prayers with tears before the Lord, and the middle of the week the Lord spoke to me and said He heard my prayers and at the end of the week I will receive my victory. Those words gave me comfort and I held on to them dearly. The Friday of that said week Garvin my first son came to see how I was doing; I couldn't hide this from him any longer so I disclose to him what I was experiencing.

The Saturday morning I decided to spend the entire day in the presence of the Lord. I showered and listened to audio Bible reading. Some time elapsed and I became sleepy so I went to lie down. I immediately dozed off and had several unclear visions. Then suddenly Jesus appeared to me and laid his two hands on my abdomen, waking up I said "I am healed!" because once the hands of Jesus touched me I knew I would no longer be the same.

As I was getting off my bed I heard Garvin's voice calling me; I said with excitement, "Son I am healed!" I related my vision to him and after listening, his expression was a happy one. Although I still felt discomfort during the day I continued to confess that I am healed.

Sunday morning I got up and had my morning devotion; then came my miracle. For the first time in two weeks the stomach discomfort was gone and I had a normal bowel movement. I worshiped God with exceeding joy that morning, recalling what I had suffered in the past. Every day of my life I give God thanks. It is now four months since I received my miracle and I am feeling great. God has given us precious promises in his word if we will only believe we will always have the victory. Thank God for His love and His mercies extended to us His Children.

12

HOPE FOR CANCER PATIENTS

There are many cancer survivors today, unlike previous years when it was like a death sentence. I lost my grandmother, one sister, and two uncles. They all succumbed to the dreaded disease. First of all our eating habits play a pivotal role and determines our life expectancy. When I was young I never made diet a priority. In fact we were very poor and I ate what was given to me. When I became an adult the foods that I relished were largely unhealthy and I believe this contributed greatly to my illness. As a result, I changed my diet completely. I refrain from eating meats, I use fish, vegetables, root crops and lots of fruits, and I also consume lots of water. The only milk I drink sometimes is Almond milk.

Living in Grenada we have various herbs at our disposal. These include Lemongrass,

Soursop leaf, Moringa, Santa Maria, Rosemary, Chadon Beni. I always enjoy a cup of hot herbal tea at bedtime. My favourite is Moringa because it is absolutely a miracle tree. Following my last surgery my blood pressure was constantly above average. One night I drank Moringa, the next morning when I checked my pressure it was normal. Exercise is also an integral part of the whole recovery process it sometime takes a strong will to get out of the house. Discipline must be exercised to ensure a healthy life style. When I think of my past illness, I always take precautionary measures to keep healthy. When I made the decision to give up meats that was a tough one, because Barbecue chicken was my favourite; but I stood my grounds and never tasted any meat since that day. Only recently, around Christmas 2013 I called a friend to find out how he was coping, he was a cancer survivor living with a colostomy. I was expecting him to answer his cell phone, but a female voice responded so I proceeded and ask for my friend. The shocking news I received I was not prepared for. She said to me "he passed away a few days ago". I took a deep breath before I found words to respond. Life is very unpredictable; we have no guarantee on our lives. Therefore, it is necessary that we be prepared to meet the Lord if we should die at any time, and that we lead a healthy lifestyle while we still have life.

I sympathise with all those who have lost their loved ones. Generally speaking I wish that everyone suffering from this disease could survive, but research has shown that not everyone does. However, there is still hope, never allow anyone's death or story to discourage you as a cancer patient. During the early stages of my recovery, many patients died but I did not dwell on that. I always strive to keep my thoughts positive. I received strength from the word of God and prayers. I also had a network of friends who kept in touch with me and gave me encouragement.

My advice to all recovering cancer patients is to practice what is right for your health. The changes that I made in my life have helped me tremendously. As a result I have made a full recovery. This would not have been possible without sacrifice. I am anticipating a long life for myself on this earth. There are so many people that need help; spiritually, financially, emotionally and otherwise. I want to make a difference in the lives of many. With God's help, all my dreams will be realised. If you have cancer or any other disease and you believe in God for healing, I have incorporated a number of scriptures which I believe will be helpful. Healing Scriptures taken from KJV.

Mark 9:23: *If thou canst believe, all things are possible to him that believeth.* Isaiah 53:5: *But he was wounded for our transgression he was bruised for our iniquities; the chastisement of our peace was upon him and with his stripes we are healed.* 3 John 1:2: *Beloved I wish above all things that thou mayest prosper and be in health, even as thy soul prospereth.*

SOME HEALING MIRACLES OF JESUS CHRIST

Luke 7:11-16: The widow's son was raised to life. Matt 9:27-31: The sights of two blind men were restored. Mark 7:31-37: A man that was deaf and mute received hearing and speech. Matt 8:5-13: The Centurion's servant was healed. John 4:46-54: Heals the Nobleman's son. John 11:1-46: Lazarus was raised from the dead. John 5:1-16: Healing of the invalid. Luke 13:10-17: The woman with the spirit of infirmity received healing.

HEALING PRAYER

Our Father who art in heaven, I exalt your holy name: I thank you Lord that healing is made possible with the stripes of Jesus Christ your son. Mark 9:23 says *all things are possible to him that believes.* Lord I believe your word and I receive healing in my body and mind in Jesus' name I pray Amen.

PREPARE FOR NEXT LIFE

In Genesis man lived for hundreds of years. Methuselah (Gen 5:27) lived nine hundred and sixty nine years. After the flood man's life expectancy was reduced to one hundred and twenty years (Gen 6:3). Later in Psalm 90:10, it reduced to seventy years. The scripture says... *and if by reason of strength we can live to eighty or more.* This simply means if we take care of our bodies having a healthy life style we can exceed three score and ten years. The obituaries on the television are sometimes appalling. The average age range of those who die is frightening. Our young people are dying. This signifies that now, more than ever before we have limited time on earth in which to prepare for life here and eternity.

We have to be cognisant of the fact that man is a spirit being living in a human body which is the temple of God. After we die there is another life, so we have to make a decision while here on earth. Hebrews 9:27 says *It is appointed on to man once to die but after this the judgement.* After death we will go to the destination based on the path that we have chosen. There are two destinations – Heaven or Hell. Based on my experience, heaven is a wonderful place and I wish that everyone will chose to go there. God does not send people to hell, people go there by choice – Rev 21:8. *The Lord is not slack concerning his promises but is long suffering towards us, and he is not willing that any should perish but that all should come to repentance* – 2 Peter 3:9 KJV. The Lord loves us unconditionally.

With human beings it is not the same. We sometimes love when everything is going well. There are people who are despised in their communities because they made a mistake along life's journey. Even if they have repented and God forgives them, Society still sees them as guilty. God is not that way, that's why he sent Jesus his son to die on the cross for us. Jesus died in our place. John 3:16 says *for God so loved the world that he gave his only begotten son that whosoever believes in him shall not perish but have eternal life.*

I have heard people say: "We have done so much evil, God will not forgive us." This is far from the truth THE BLOOD OF JESUS CLEANSES US FROM ALL OUR SINS.

When we are blessed in this earthly life, we should not shut up our bowels of compassion. God has blessed us so we in turn could be a blessing to others. I am not implying that we must not enjoy the fruit of our labour but we must bear in mind that the earth is the Lord's and the fullness thereof, and if riches should increase we should not set our hearts upon it – Psalm 62:10 KJV.

The Lord appeared to me in a vision one night. At that time I was in a foreign land and I was going through some prosecution. I was at the point of giving up, I remembered going and lay down to die. Suddenly, I saw the lord in the sky with his hands out stretched! I looked up at him and said, "Lord you are up there and I am down here." The Lord then came down and I was walking side by side with him in green pastures. We were both walking in silence, but his presence made the difference. A knock on my bedroom door that night interrupted that vision. When I got up I felt refreshed and strengthened, and had no desire to die again.

If you are reading this book and you don't know Jesus as your Saviour, take a few minutes and talk to him. He is waiting to hear from you. Just ask him to forgive all your sins and come into your heart. It does not matter what you have done in the past. Jesus will forgive you. God is real and his word is true that's why I am alive today to share my story.

Life is a journey we have no blueprints to follow so we have to trust God to lead us. We will make mistakes but we have to learn by them. I have been on my journey for a while I have learned humility and to wait on the Lord. I have experienced disappointments and discouragements. I remembered Job when his sufferings became extreme he cursed the day he was born – Job 3:1. I now understand why he did so. You will never understand what another person is going through unless you experience it yourself.

I had many other encounters with the Lord which I will share in another book. God is love, God is real. He is the best friend we could ever have. Whenever you are discouraged and you don't know where to turn, look up – your heavenly Father is only a prayer away.

◉

ABOUT THE AUTHOR

Apostle Rachel is an ordained minister of the Gospel. She is also the founder of Trinity Hall Ministries, where she laboured tirelessly until the time of her illness. She has a passion for the lost and the less fortunate. Though tested and tried she remains steadfast and is determined to complete the race she has started. *Pastor N Auguste, 2015*

16194307R00079

Printed in Poland
by Amazon Fulfillment
Poland Sp. z o.o., Wrocław